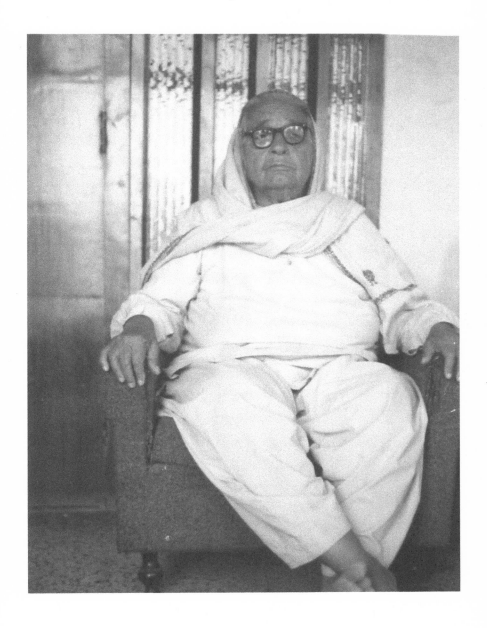

THE BIOGRAPHY OF HOLY WOMAN BIBI LAJO

A Perfect Disciple

R.K. Rajput

ISBN: 978-1-4834-2103-2 (sc)
ISBN: 978-1-4834-2104-9 (e)

Lulu Publishing Services rev. date: 12/09/2014

INTRODUCTION

How was I able to find this holy woman?

In 1952 when I had my summer vacations from the school in Amritsar, I was living with my parents in Punjab state in India when I saw a book lying on the table. When I opened the book I read something about Hazur Sawan Singh (the Great Master of Beas.) The book's name was <u>Sakhian,</u> which means "the travels." This was the right time in my life to start reading such a book. Day by day I was taking interest to read every story in the book. I went through the book twice. There are about sixty five stories of Hazur's travels written by Bibi Lajo, who herself was traveling with Hazur. She wrote so as to keep the memories of her beloved Master fresh and to pass her time in the separation from her Guru.

This book held something in store for me. When I finished the book, it inspired me so much that I thought the writer of the book was the Mira Bai of today. When I read it the third time, I thought about the writer. Who was she and what was her address? I found the address on the second page and was so glad to know that the writer lived in the same city I lived in, which was Amritsar (Punjab.) But the distance was about five miles too far to walk from my house. So, the next day I took my bicycle and went to her house. She was very happy to see me. I told her how I was inspired by her stories. I sat in the room in which she had arranged Hazur's belongings everywhere. Hazur's bed was decorated. On the pillow Hazur's original painting was lying. I bowed my head and touched Hazur's shoes and the wooden shoes of Baba Jaimal Singhji. I found myself lucky to have the darshan ("to look at") all of the belongings of Hazur. She brought a glass full of fresh milk and asked me to drink it. She told me that the milk is fresh from the calf of Hazur's own cow, which he had given to her. She raised the calf herself and brought it along with her to Amritsar. I drank the milk and found myself lucky to have the parshad (blessed food) from such a holy woman. I told her, "I go to Beas Dera with my parents and all of my brothers and sisters stay in the Dera during our holidays and then we do sewa (service) by carrying baskets of soil on our heads after which we usually go to langar (food or food hall) and cook the chapattis (similar to tortillas) and clean the utensils." She was very impressed by me and advised me to visit her regularly. I sat with her for two hours and listened to the stories of Hazur. She was telling the stories with nonstop tears pouring from her eyes. I was surprised to see her condition and thought what kind of love and devotion she had for her Guru who had made her condition like that. And what type of love was that which made her so pained that she did not stop shedding tears, even for a second. From one eye to the other she was wiping one eye and the other was shedding again and again and never stopped. When I came back home I was thinking and thinking and I wanted to be with her. When I went to see her the next day, I told her that I wanted to be with her. She said I could stay with her forever. From that day forward there was hardly a day that I did not visit her. So day-by-day months and years passed, visiting her and enjoying her holy company. I used to travel with her until the end of her last journey and I sat in the ambulance sent by the great Master Charan Singh Maharaj Ji. Her last journey ended in the holy place of the Dera Beas where her Guru the great Hazur had left her. There are a lot of things to write about her and her love given to the sangat and me, so that the readers can know her from her own biography, written by this slave.

Thank You
R.K. Rajput.

CHILDHOOD

Bibi Lajo herself said that when she was eight years old she died and her parents kept her dead body at home for one day and one night. The next day when her dead body was taken to the graveyard it was all wrapped in the coffin. Her dead body was placed on the wooden pyre in order to cremate it. All her kith and kin including her parents were standing around the grave. All of a sudden her body started moving and all the relatives except her uncle and aunt ran away thinking her a ghost. The uncle untied the cloth and she sat down. He took her in his lap. At that time her face was red and she was smiling. Her parents came back to take their child back from her uncle's house. But they did not give the child back because they told that she was left by them. Her uncle said, "She does not belong to you anymore." Her uncle and aunt then raised her. She did not go back to her parents. Her uncle and aunt were very rich and they did not have their own child. She was married at the age of eleven. She told me that when the marriage party and her father in law were on their way to the home, that she was sitting in special kind of doli, which is the Indian traditional carrier for the bride. On the way she saw some girls of her age who were playing near a well. When she saw them she pretended to be thirsty so that she could be allowed to get out of the doli. Her father in law let her get down to drink some water from the well. She ran to the girls and started to play with them.

The father in law picked her up in his arms and made her sit in the doli and gave her water to drink. She explained to me how she was innocent about marriage at that age. She made me laugh with her innocent stories of her childhood. Four men pulled her doli. She was wearing bride's clothes and a lot of ornaments made of gold. People from the groom's family were riding on horses and the bridegroom was riding on an elephant which was decorated with gaudy clothes. When she saw the beautiful elephant she told the carriers of her doli that she wanted to sit on the elephant but she was wearing a long veil and she was not allowed to show her face to the bridegroom. In those days child marriage was in vogue, so some members of her parent's family were also going with her as she went to her in laws' house. She was brought back to her parent's house the next day by the members of her parent's family. In this way she was staying in her uncle's house when she became a widow at the age of twelve, but she did not know the meaning of being a widow. She loved her beautiful clothes and the jewelry. The widow was supposed to wear white clothes in those days according to social rules. Her friends were trying to stop her from wearing those beautiful clothes and the ornaments, but she did not stop until she turned fifteen. She came to know what being a widow meant. She started wearing the white clothes and kept on wearing them until the end of her life. When she left her body in 1984 she was still wearing the white clothes.

After she turned fifteen she started visiting the temple in her village and she learned all about the spiritual stories of Rama and Lord Krishna. She believed in having fasts to please the gods and goddesses. Slowly and slowly the ladies from that area started to listen to her holy songs in praise of the gods and goddesses. She used to read the holy books, The Ramayana and The Gita, everyday. She used to do satsang at home and the ladies used to come to her house to listen to her satsang. She kept on doing all of that until she met the Great Master Sawan Singh Maharaj Ji.

The method she had chosen to worship and to become a true devotee to Lord Krishna was very wonderful. She told how she would put her whole attention and love to make her Lord Krishna happy. I was very much surprised at her way of doing simran. She told that she would tear a paper and make many little pieces. Then she picked the pieces up and wrote the name of Krishna on the piece of paper and she would make a little ball and put that into a small basket. She kept on doing this for hours and hours everyday at her fixed time. When the basket was full she would put them in a sack and when the sack was full she would place the sack into a room which she had made only for the sacks. Day by day, month by month and year by year she kept on doing this. Then she stopped eating salt for eleven years. When she met Hazur she was still on this fast. She had tattoos of Lord Krishna on both of her arms and OM on her hand. Her back also had a tattoo of Krishna. All the ladies loved her very much and believed that she herself was a goddess. In the company of the ladies of the area she used to celebrate the birthday of Lord Krishna.

MEETING HAZUR
IN HER VILLAGE

As the soul was already prepared for the Lord's house, Hazur visited her village and had a satsang there. Some of the women went to Hazur and told him about her spirituality. When Hazur heard about this he sent someone to get her, but she did not come. So, Hazur went to see her. She welcomed Hazur but did not agree to follow his path. Before leaving her place, Hazur told her to visit Beas. One day the same ladies went to ask her if she wanted to go to Beas with them and she agreed. When she was leaving, her aunt advised her not to see her mother in Jullundur because she would never let her go to Beas. So, she went straight to Beas with her friends. After listening to Hazur's satsang she was very impressed but she went back to her village with her friends. The next month Hazur went to give satsang in her village and sent her a message to come to the satsang but she could not go because of restrictions by her aunt and uncle. They did not want her to meet the saints as they feared she might leave them and would go with the saint. So Hazur went to see her again and asked her whom she was worshipping. She told him about the Lord Krishna and showed a lot of love for Him. She showed the room where she had kept her Lord Krishna in the sacks. Hazur laughed and said, "Your Lord Krishna needs fresh air

and a good place to live." She was very innocent and loved her Lord
Krishna. She was very happy to hear this and agreed with Hazur.
Saying this Hazur left. She kept on fasting and worshipping the gods
and was busy in doing satsangs of Ramayana and The Gita. One day
she was celebrating the birthday of Lord Krishna and some ladies
sitting close to her were saying, "This holy woman, if she lived in
Beas then she would be fortunate to see Hazur every day and she
would be the holiest one." She heard them talking about Hazur. She
asked them, "What are you talking about?" They told her that Hazur
himself is God. She asked why God would come on the Earth? They
replied, "You can ask Hazur yourself." She said, "All right, I would
like to go to Beas with you after this celebration." The next day she
finished the satsang and the havan (worship of the fire goddess) and
she went to ask her aunt Kesardevi, who was a very conservative
woman. She advised her not to go because she did not want to send
a young girl out of the house to live in holy places. She answered her
aunt that she was going to see the great saint and not thieves. The
rest of the family members did not know that she was going to see
the saint as only her aunt knew. This time she was determined to see
Hazur. So, she told her aunt that she must go even though her aunt
would not allow her and somehow she convinced her aunt to let her
go. The name of God was echoing in her mind. She was questioning
herself, "If God is on the Earth then why am I at home?" "Was I
meant to be with him?" She told her aunt, "*Mira Bai* left her palace
and went to see the saints?" After this she immediately left with her
friends for Beas. On the way she stopped in her real mother's house
at Jullundur. Her real mother's name was Bhagwati. She told her that
she was going to meet 'the saint from Beas.' Her mom became very
happy and called her the luckiest one. She asked her if she could go
with her. This time everything was in her favor because Hazur was

taking care of her. As soon as she heard the happy words from her mom, she left the house quickly with her friends. She reached the railway station to catch the train for Beas, which was hardly forty miles away from Jullundur. It took one hour to reach Beas. It was 3:00 p.m. when she reached Beas and went straight to Hazur's room, but the door was closed. So she decided to sit near his room which was next to the room where <u>Guru Granth Sahib</u> was kept (the holy book of the ten Sikh Gurus.) The other two girls who came along with her, Uwari and Rampiyari also sat with her. They told her, "When Hazur comes out of his room you can try to touch his feet. But, if he stops her then she should not feel bad as Hazur doesn't allow anyone to do this." She replied, "It doesn't matter because I understand that the perfect saints have certain limits."

At 4:00 p.m. Hazur came out. He was wearing his eyeglasses and had a white shawl on his shoulders. His appearance attracted her. She was surprised to see his charming personality and majestic gait. Looking at his face her inner eye was opened and she could see Hazur as God. Hazur went to her directly. He placed his hand on her head and asked her lovingly, "My dear daughter, why did you take so long to come here?" She replied, "I was able to come only when you called me." She placed her head on his feet and touched them. On this he laughed and said to her, "Come with me and let's do the satsang." She said to Hazur, "I have not come to do the satsang, but I have come to listen to your satsang." Hazur said, "No, you are here to do the satsang." This was her first meeting in the Dera with him and she received the extended grace from Hazur.

Bibi Lajo was still fasting at the time when she came to see Hazur in Beas. When Hazur was doing satsang, he started to explain about her life and her fasts. She was surprised to know how Hazur knew everything about her life as she had never explained anything to him before. Hazur looked at her and started telling all of the previous events of her life since her birth. He said, "It was the game of the two dolls; one belongs to the spiritual life and the other belongs to the materialistic life, but their clothes are still clean. The pot is empty and it needs something to keep in it." After the satsang he directly went to her and said, "Oh my daughter! Let's go to our home." She said, "I have to go back to my home today." Hazur said, "Sure, I will take you to your home." Saying this Hazur brought her to his residence. He called another bibi ("lady") and said to her, "Bibi Lajo has come from Jullundur. Serve her with food from my kitchen. She is a very precious soul and take proper care of her." Then he said that she is a good example of a lover of God. Then he told Bibi Lajo, "Nobody will ask you anything and you will have your own importance in this house." Saying this he went to his room and called his servant, Sohan. He said, "Bring the bibi who has come from Jullundur." When the servant came to her and said that Hazur was calling her in his room, she refused to go because she had never been in a room alone with a man. The servant went back to Hazur and told that she didn't want to come. Hazur was very happy to know that and he himself came to her and said, "My daughter, saints and sadhus have nothing to do with the worldly activities. They only deal with the loving souls. So, think as if you are with your father and come with me." She went with Hazur and with the other bibis along with the servant in his room. She told Hazur about her spiritual life and wept that she wanted to see God and the inner world, where she belongs. Hazur said, "Don't worry my daughter, you will see everything inside. That is why you are here."

The very next day she was initiated by the Great Master Hazur Sawan Singh Ji. She learned the words of the holy mantra very quickly and Hazur made her sit for meditation, giving her all the instructions. She followed them in no time. In this first meditation

Hazur took her in the inner planes and made her sit in the sound meditation from 4:00 p.m. to 7:00 p.m. He gave her full satisfaction in knowing the inner world about which she was interested. After this she had firm faith in her Perfect Master and Guru. After that she was a perfect disciple for her loving Master and Guru until the end of her life.

Hazur asked her to attend his satsangs every month. She told Hazur that her relatives are orthodox and they will not allow her to come again. Then she asked how it would be possible to see him again. Hazur laughed and said lovingly, "Kako, you are destined to spend your life with me while I am here in this world." She was surprised to hear Hazur's words and went back to her house after spending six days in Hazur's company. These words of Hazur were echoing in her mind continuously. Thinking about these words she was overwhelmed with joy. When she came to her house she came to know that her uncle was transferred to Amritsar, which is the city located next to Jullundur. In between both these cities, Beas railway station comes on the way. So she was very happy to know this news and hoped to visit her Guru in his Dera. Her uncle told her to come with him to Amritsar. She quickly agreed to go and was very happy because Beas was on the way to Amritsar. She planned to get out of the train in Beas station to see Hazur when the train stopped there. But her aunt knew of her plans so she told her husband to go by express train which would not stop at the Beas railway station. He made reservations for the express train. They reached Amritsar without stopping at Beas, but on the way back by the same train, Bibi Lajo started doing simran (repetition of holy words.) In her simran she requested that her Master give her his darshan (a view of the Master's face.) So, when the train reached closer to Beas railway station, the signal was not given to the train and the train had to stop.

As soon as the train stopped she jumped out of the train pretending that she was thirsty and she wanted to drink some water. Her aunt was calling her name loudly but she was drinking water. She went on drinking water until the train started to move fast. She was left there and she straight away went to the Dera. Hazur was sitting in the chair in his yard as if he was waiting for someone. When Bibi Lajo came she touched the feet of her Master. Hazur laughed and said, "Kako, you were saying that you can't come again, so how come you have made it now?" Then he said, "You were praying so hard to have darshan that your Satguru had to listen to you."

After that day she never went back home. All her relatives made many plans to bring her back but she never went back to her house. She lived in the house which was given to her by "her Hazur." She was destined to live in this house for the rest of her life. Later, all her relatives became satsangies and were blessed by Hazur. They were shown so many miracles by Hazur that were unexplainable. All of her life was spent in the service of Hazur until he left his body.

After Hazur left his body, she spent some days in Beas. Then she decided to come to Amritsar satsangghar where her Master used to visit. During his lifetime, she was doing every job for him at this place. She was very attached to his belongings that were in this satsangghar. She was allowed to have all of these belongings by the current great Satguru, Sardar Bahadur Maharaj Ji in Beas Dera. All the satsangies could understand the pains and sufferings of her separation from "her Guru."

Kirpal Singh Maharaj Ji, who was equally going through the same kind of pains and suffering for Hazur like Bibi Lajo came to see his "Nanaki", sister Bibi Lajo. He along with Bibi Lajo had spent years together in Hazur's service in Beas. He took the responsibility to work with her in the sweet memory of "their Master." Sant Kirpal

Singh Maharaj Ji loved and respected Bibi Lajo as his sister. So when he started his Master's work and became Master he bought the land for his Guru sister, Bibi Lajo in front of his satsangghar in Amritsar. He knew she was attached to the loving sangat of Amritsar. She liked to spend the rest of her life doing satsang in the memory of her beloved Master and celebrating his birthday as well as his days of departure. On these occasions she invited Satguru Kirpal Singh Ji to do satsang and invited all the senior government officers along with their families to have langar (food) at her own residence. She prepared langar by hiring the satsangie cooks which everyone used to enjoy. I myself attended the satsangs in their company and did sewa (service) along with her according to her directions. She is the one who inspired me to have the grace of my Satguru and she is the one who always stood by me. She was my spiritual mother. I traveled with her wherever she was invited by the Masters and their loving satsangies. She always was happy to have me with her. She introduced me to the loving satsangies and gave me the happiness in my life.

By her kind favor I used to visit her every day in the morning before going to my college and later to my job. Sometime by the end of the day, I sat with her to listen to the intoxicated nonstop stories of Hazur. Hours used to pass by when she told stories of Hazur. During this time many satsangies would come, sit, and enjoy her stories and leave. She had nonstop tears in her eyes while telling these stories. Wherever she went with me she started the stories of her beloved and made everybody intoxicated in such a way that everybody would forget to leave the place. If I start to explain everything, I think it would be endless and moreover I have no word to explain her spiritual beauty and greatness with which she graced everyone. Sometimes she would sing in a loud and melodious voice the songs in praise of her beloved Master and sometimes she would sing the shabads in the grief of His memory. The pangs of separation from her Guru were really unbearable and inexpressible. Everybody who met her would be a true witness of her story telling and that she never forgot her beloved Guru until she left her body. In other words she never stopped remembering her Master from the day she met him until the last breath of her life. I was with her until the last moments of her journey to her beloved Satguru.

MEMORIES OF SAWAN (PENNED BY BIBI LAJO HERSELF)

(TRANSLATED AND UNEDITED)

The actual wordings of shabads are written in the Hindi language. For the readers of this book, I am translating her words into English. I have made my best attempt to translate these words from Hindi to English. Since the exact beauty described within these words is in Hindi, I feel sorry that I may not be able to translate completely her words. But her autobiography she communicated to me and I wrote in my diary side by side.

Shabad

Oh, my friends this is the month of Sawan (July) all the flowers are blooming in the garden so please do not pluck them. In Sawan there is greenery everywhere. When my Lord Sawan was in his physical form all the flowers were laughing, but now they look like they are faded.

The mother Jiwani (the name of Hazur's mother) was the great who gave birth to my Lord Sawan. The father Kabul Singh is great who played with my Lord Sawan. All were making marries on his birthday and the world came to know about his power. Baba Jaimal was the great who found my Lord in Kala Bagh in the mountains Himalayas and brought the Diamond in Beas Dehra. On the bank of river Beas he gave the wealth of Naam to everyone "Radha Soami Din Dyal Ki Dya Radha Soami Sahaya." He gave us the chain of separation to wear around our neck, giving us a lot of love and encouragement. He left all of us in the middle of deep river of life.

Oh, my dear Lord I have never had a single thought of your separation like this and never had a single idea of facing such troubles in my life. Only nineteen days were left when my Satguru looked at me with his pitiful eyes. Putting me in the illusion of love he started to say some words, "Look my child, I feel pity on you what will happen to you when I'll be gone."

"I will soon throw this body. Nobody will take care of you. You will cry here and there you will not see my face. There will be all darkness around you. You will sob and remember me."

Then I replied to my lord, "Please send me to the Sachkhand before you leave me."

My Satguru replied, "I cannot do anything before the order of my Satguru. If my Satguru places the knife on disciple's neck what the disciple can do and how can the disciple refuse.

I again requested to be my attorney and say to your Satguru that there was no one to take care of your child. How would be able to see me again? My Satguru said, "Talk as much as you can today, there will be no one to listen to you after I am gone. I will change this building the time I go and you will cry for me in the rest of your life. One day I will come to take you, and then you'll be free from the services that you have to do for the sangat. But for now you have to teach them the meaning of life. How to live in the pains miseries of being separated from the Master."

I again requested, "I will drink the poison and die. I want to go with you." Then my Lord gave strict order not to do that and rejected my request. I again said, "I would not be able to have your physical darshan in my life. How would I be able to spend my life?" Being very kind he said, "May Satpurush will call you soon or he will shower his grace upon you to live the rest of your life in my memory." After talking with me he was lost inside and closed his eyes. He finally decided to leave all of us and broke my heart leaving me crying and sobbing behind. For nineteen days before he left us he talked to me everyday and night in the presence of Sant Kirpal Singh Ji. Thursday night he turned his face from all of us for ever. That was the dark day of 2nd April. The next day on Friday 3rd April MY LORD started his final journey to Sachkhand leaving the world mourning and wailing for him. When my Satguru left the worldly home, my whole body was trembling and side by side all the buildings were looking like shattering filled with sounds of the cries from his loved ones. Hai (TAKING THE DEEP SIGH!) the sharp sword of separation pierced in the center of my heart. I could see nothing. There were all dark clouds spreading before my tearful eyes. His grief occupied my heart and storm of dark life was coming for me. Everybody in Dera was crying, mourning and wailing. The young, the elders, the children and everyone were in shock. To me even the birds, the cattle and the trees were looking in shock. The wind started to slow down. MY BEAUTIFUL LORD was sitting on the chair and was being brought down by the stairs from his palace by the sewadars. He said final farewell to his temple and never would go upstairs as for which he used to. He will never enter his room and would call me for food. All the loved ones made my Satguru ready quickly. They did not let any body stay by him. It was a blowing storm for me when they were making him ready to leave the temple. I walked behind my Lord crying and wailing. Nobody let me look at his face even for a single time again. My all the hopes were dashed to the ground. There was no one to listen to me. The days were filled with all kinds of troubles and suffering for me. I passed thirteen days with difficulties. After final ceremony the crown was broken. After fifteen days, I left for the home where my Lord used to go, the city of Amritsar. Hoping that my Satguru could be seen in the home where he used to stay and do the monthly satsang and felt very happy to stay there. But he was not seen there also. I was doing simran and was sitting on meditation for long time but here was fire burning in my heart to see him physically. The memories of his physical form were still fresh, so in meditation my eyes remained wet with tears. On fifteenth days he left the body, I did Bhandara and the final sewa from my side in his home. Like before, I heard no voice of my Satguru. After twenty five days, I again went to Dera Beas. I was wandering like mad person thinking where I should stay and which place was left for me to live in the memory of my Satguru. This time I was crying and crying, Satguru did not give darshan or called me Kako. I heaved long and deep sighs but I could not find my Lord. Then I decided to go to Sirsa, the city of my Lord. Everybody from his family was there but only the glittering face of my Lord was not seen. My heart was broken. The body was as light as the light of the moon. At night when I was sobbing in his memory, my Lord appeared in form of shabad. After giving darshan he disappeared and my heart was broken again. I was not used to miss him like that. So I came back to Dera Beas again. But I was refused to stay there. This is the same Dera Beas where I was brought up by my Lord, where I lived in the world of joys sharing happiness with my Lord. There was no place for me to stay then. That was a very difficult time for me to choose the place anywhere else in the world. Only my Satguru was there to decide for the place to live for me. I could not express myself before anyone what to do. I always remained at the disposal of my Satguru for all the life. I stayed with him. I never had thought of this day before. I did not have the time to think about such kind of life or the separation of my Lord. The Dera which gave the life and the pleasures of my Satguru services had no place for me to stay. I was hungry since morning and night for the food as well as for the love of my Sachepatshah. So when I felt myself in the state of unwanted person in the physical presence of my Lord. I made up my mind not to stay and leave house of my Satguru's which was built in my presence. My Satguru accepted sewa of my wedding ornaments for the construction of Sachkhand. I also did physical sewa for the Sachkhand when it was constructed. Now this is the same place where I was not allowed to live. With this disappointment and bearing a lot of load of troubles in my heart, I left the Dera without having plans for rest of my life. The only feeling was the faith in my Guru who was always with me and would remain with me. He would make better plan for me to lead the rest of my life. So again I went back to Amritsar with guidance of my Lord living inside with me. The crown which was given to me by my Satguru to wear for service of the sangat was taken away from me. When I came in satsangghar of Amritsar, I felt like a fish without water. I kept on crying for days and nights thinking what to do? How to live my life without my Lord? One night, the sleep took over me. In my dreams, I was still crying and talking to my Lord questioning why he snatched the lap in which I played like a child? When I woke up, I thought of going to Dalhousie in the lap of Himalayas. This is the place where my Satguru used to stay and I was fortunate to cook his food and do his sewa.

When I went to Dalhousie and opened the house where my Satguru was living all the memories surrounded me and made me cry again. I could not control my tears when I saw the room and the other belongings of my Satguru lying there. It was for the first time I came without the company of my Lord. I spend the whole night in tears. In the morning, I went to the forest to see if I could have his darshan there. When I reached there, I felt, as if my Lord was playing hide and seek with me. Sometime, I felt as if he is present, but sometimes he disappeared. After sometime, I could not decide how long I should stay there? My heart was burning like a hot plate. I didn't want to see those trees and flowers, which once had them spring when my Lord was visiting there. But now everything was looking as autumn to me. There was still rain of tears coming through my eyes. I was lost in the memories of how I used to decorate his room with flowers? I was just like a lost child, who was looking for his lost father. This was my real condition. I can't even describe it completely. No one can understand my condition at that time until someone is blessed by his Master's love and separation, especially with the Master like Sawan Singh. I was washed away with strong waves of my tears. I am writing this book and my eyes are still wet with tears. I hardly could see the paper. I am wiping my eyes after writing every word. These are the non-stop tears in the memory of my Lord. I have the bed of thorns in the room of my heart where I would like to sleep on so that I could feel the severe pain of separation. I would love to be in the state of suffering which could make his memories fresh and the tear would remind me his loving words.

"You [My Lord] gave the life of roses and now the life of thorns.
Thank You my lord! But in both ways you are with me.
You are my protector for the rest of my life."

I remember Mira Bai who wrote, "In the game of such kind of life if she is defeated she will belong to her Lord; if she is the winner then the Lord will belong to her." So, loving meeting and the pangs of separation will be for both of us but I have already surrendered myself to my Guru. He give me strength to live the life of separation and then take me to his new house.

One devotee came to me and asked me why I was sitting there alone and crying for the departed Master he advised me to go with him. I locked my Satguru's house and came with him thinking that if I survived, I'll come back. He helped me to catch the bus to Amritsar. The night went on with sobbing and having tears in my eyes. He also accompanied me and on the way he took care of me. We reached satsangghar of Amritsar and talked about the loving Lord and the whole day went in his memory. The storm of sorrows would not let me sleep at night. On one side the darkness of sorrows and on the other side the night itself was dark and the moreover the heart was filled with worries of spending the rest of my life without him. Thoughts of his memories were eating me. Especially to see how the land was barren in his absence? There was not even a single car or the horse cart. This is the same place which was filled with cars and with thousands of people around. The month of Sawan was itself sad without Sawan. No color of henna on my hands, no swinging on the trees (as in the month of Sawan the girls swing on the trees now no one is swinging.) I didn't even want my friends (Bibi was remembering those days of Sawan when ladies used to put henna on there hands and make marries by swinging on the branches of the trees. But that was the month of sorrows for her in the memory of her Satguru.)

Now all my satsangi friends come to me and cry for the same reason. I never had a dream that such a day will come during month

19

of Sawan. In this month, all of the people used to come from far away to celebrate the birthday of my Lord and enjoyed a huge treat. They made marries by listening his satsang and singing the shabads in his praise. Now all those memories are stinging me like a sting of the black snakes. All were doing sewa with love and devotion. Now my Lord Sawan would never come back in the month of Sawan. Oh God! Nobody should face such a time of separation by his dear one. Where are you hiding? Nobody was sharing my sorrows.

It would be good that I would have died before you left me. The dew drops on the lilies and the roses are crying for you. They are missing you. They used to laugh when you were sitting by them. You were the most beautiful Master of all. You had a majestic gait and charming personality on this Earth. His pink lips and the smile on them with bright beard on the face was killing everyone and his graceful eyes were intoxicating everyone. Anyone who kept his company would forget his troubles and sufferings. They would never like to leave him. When somebody stood close to him, they felt the smell and the fragrance of jasmine, sandal and the roses. Then those who were standing at a distance would feel the same too. I would have not given my heart to him, if I knew that he was going to leave me in lurch.

I am writing your songs in the burning memories of yours and crying but everybody is busy with their families and work. My life would be spent telling your loving stories and praising you with the company you give it to me of your loving devotees. My life will be spent on your name and I'll die having your name on my breath (which was true when Bibi left.)

In the end of this shabad she wrote, "His picture is merged in my body like the redness in henna."

(END SHABAD OF BIBI LAJO)

This was all she wrote in the memory of Hazur and explained the pains she had from the separation of her Guru. She expressed in a very beautiful way using poetic words written in Hindi.

Bibi Lajo was educated up to the primary school during the days when the British ruled over India. She knew how to write and read in Hindi. She had a very loud voice when she was singing shabads in praise of her Master. She would shed tears and sang his shabads. I myself have heard her many times. Her sad songs would make everyone cry. When I met her she had a big room where she kept all the belongings of Hazur. She had decorated the room very nicely. She had Hazur's bed and would change the bed sheet as usual, like the way she used to do when Hazur was physically present. Then she had fixed the roof on the bed with white silk cloth and placed the small bulbs of multi colored light. In the room she had Hazur's shoes and Baba Jaimal Singh's wooden shoes and placed them on the stool made of silver and sandal wood. She placed them by the bed where Hazur used to keep them that he can step on it before getting on his bed. On the head of the bed there was Hazur's pillow and in the middle of the bed there was a big cushion, where she placed the hand made painting of Hazur. The painting was drawn by a foreign painter. He had his signature on the bottom of the painting. Hazur was requested by the painter to sit for four hours everyday for forty days in front of him to create this master piece. The painting was kept in a wooden frame. It was so attractive that one can feel as if Hazur himself is looking at you. The painting was placed by the cushion on his bed. She had a chair with one arm and one round shaped table that belonged to Hazur. She also had a round shaped pot made of silver with a thin lid on it. She used to fill the pot with water at night and used to sit for meditation believing that Hazur will come and will drink the water. In the morning she used to check the pot and noticed the water level was reduced by one inch. So she used to believe that Hazur had come and drank the water from the pot. Actually, when Hazur was present, she used to serve him with water from the same pot. Later, when Hazur left his body we drank some water from that pot treating it as Amrit (nectar.) Everyone liked to have the water from her from this pot. She herself used to give some drops of water to everyone who went to listen to Hazur's stories. This was the daily routine for the satsangies living in the city. She would serve everyone with the tea and some cookies and food. She did her duty to serve the loving devotees of Hazur. There was no fixed time to visit her. Anyone could come and visit her anytime. She was always surrounded by the satsangies starting from morning until late at night. People used to sit for hours and enjoyed the intoxicating stories of Hazur. She used to tell these stories non-stop in a series for hours. Some of the stories made people laugh and cry. The low and the high, the poor and the rich, everyone used to visit her. Even the chief secretary of the Punjab state of India, the commissioner's of the cities, the judges and their families, the deputy commissioners of police and their families; all used to visit her and listen to her stories. They attended the big treats of Hazur's celebration of his birthdays and his departure days. All the celebrations used to take place at her residence in Amritsar city, which is forty miles away from Beas Dera where Hazur used to live and she would always be with Hazur doing his sewa day and night.

So, all those with high ranks were also brought up in the lap of Hazur and in her company because the families of these officers were dwelling in Beas Dera. Some were the writers of the books and some of them were managing everything in Beas Dera. They had their own little world in the company of their Great Master Sawan Singh Maharaj Ji. It felt as if he was still living there doing satang and constructing the satsangghar and giving guidance for construction.

Hazur himself was an engineer in the military during the time when the British ruled in India. So he knew how to construct the buildings as well as to build the spiritual building of life. People who enjoyed Bibi's company in the presence of Hazur had loved her as a perfect devotee of Hazur. Even Hazur's family had a great respect for her. If the satsangies had any celebration at their house, such as marriages or opening new business etc., they used to come and pick her up for the ceremony and to receive blessings from her. She had a heart full of love, generosity and gratefulness. She was a very calm and happy soul. She had her own spiritual beauty on her face and in her personal nature. She was very innocent and loving. Sometimes if she uttered some words as blessings, they would come true. For example, if someone asked for a son, she would give her flower to the lady with the name of Hazur and would say, "Okay, Hazur will do it. Do not worry, he is always with us." Saying so, she would laugh. I myself used to write the date and the day of the month for the people who visited her in order to record the result of her blessing. To my surprise, after a year the same ladies would come with their little babies to get a name from Bibi. She would laugh and say, "See! My Hazur listens to everybody. He is very generous and kind to his devotees."

Most of my life I traveled with her whenever she had to go in or out of town. She always got me to keep her company during her travels. I was also very fortunate to be in the grace of my Master to travel along with her and took care of her during her journey and stayed in the satsangghars or in the satsangies houses. For me it was a good opportunity to do sewa for the highest and most loving soul of Hazur. My parents would never stop me. They were very happy and always allowed me to go with her.

Once, our family and Bibi Lajo were staying in Delhi at Sawan Ashram. I was seventeen years old. Satguru Kirpal Singh Ji came to our room and told Bibi that satsangies from Khuraja town wanted to take her to their town for the wedding ceremony of their daughter. She said, "How can I [Bibi] go alone like this? I am not feeling well and I have a bad cough and cold." My Satguru Dins Dyal [Kirpal Singh Ji Maharaj] answered, "Why are you worried? I am sending my daughter Raj with you. She will take care of you and give you medicine. You will be okay." After he said this, Satguru Ji left the room. The satsangies who knew Bibi since Hazur's time came in the room. I wore an old dress and didn't have any other dress because we left Amritsar during the war between India and Pakistan. We had to leave the city in a day. The whole city was evacuated by the government. So, we couldn't bring many clothes with us. My mom was a little scared to send her young daughter to unknown people and spend the night there. But my Satguru noticed her and said, "Look, I am her father and she is the daughter of a Lion (the surname "Singh" in Punjabi means "Lion") so you forget the ideas you are having and stay happy. She has to go in order to take care of Bibi." I remember how my Satguru was looking straight into the eyes of my mom and he was also facing my dad. He asked my dad if he was right. My dad laughed and folded his hand and said that she was definitely his daughter. My Satguru gave a beautiful smile to my dad and held my hand. He said, "Are you happy now?" I touched his lotus feet. He patted me on my back and then placed his right hand on my head and ordered me to sit in the car with Bibi. In the evening we made it to Khuraja. I had never seen this part of the country before. These people were the owners of a screw factory. They were very rich people and gave us nice rooms with good looking beds. I was surprised to see the room and the beds.

After dinner the tailor came in to take my dress size and then left. Bibi was making fun of me. She said, "Now you will have good looking clothes to wear for the wedding. I'll see how you look in those bright dresses." I had been wearing very simple dresses in my student life, so Bibi was making fun of me. She was very happy. In the morning two dresses were given to me to wear. I tried them on and they fit right on me. In the evening two more dresses were given to me. They were very beautiful dresses. When I wore them, Bibi was very happy to see me in the dresses. The girls of the family came to make me ready to attend the marriage. Bibi was also with me and we enjoyed the wedding. After the wedding, Bibi and I were visiting many people. Everyday everyone wanted to have Bibi's blessings. We visited the houses and Bibi did the satsang. We sang the shabads (songs) of Hazur and had a good time. After ten days we came back to Sawan Ashram. She blessed so many ladies with their sons. I was surprised when they visited Bibi in Amritsar bringing their children. They stayed for ten days. I had a good opportunity to serve them in Bibi's residence as this was my home town.

MEETING WITH SATGURU KIRPAL SINGH MAHARAJ JI

Bibi Lajo was the Nanaki sister of Nanak Kirpal Singh Ji Maharaj. She used to call him brother Nanak. They used to sit and talk about Hazur in his room at her residence where all of the sangat used to have their darshan. They looked very beautiful. I remember the time when Bibi Lajo and Sant Kirpal Singh Ji Maharaj were sitting together. I used to sit very close to Bibi, listening to their conversation and enjoying the darshan of my Satguru Ji. One day Bibi came back from the hospital after having eye surgery. Master Kirpal Ji also came to see her. While they were talking some sewadars and I were listening to them. Bibi was saying "When we go to Sachkhand to live with Hazur, we would leave on the same day and at the same time but there will be an interval of ten years between us." As usual, I wrote these words in my diary. When the time came there was definitely a ten year interval and the time matched. It was exactly correct.

Both Bibi Lajo and Kirpal Singh Ji Maharaj left the physical body to live with their Master in Sachkhand. We should not have any doubt in it. It doesn't make a difference if the soul is in a male or a female's body. When it comes in the form of a saint, it guides us. Saints give us good directions and signs but it is very hard to recognize the living Master without his grace.

Once, my dad fell sick with typhoid. He was admitted in the police hospital in Amritsar for three months. He was getting weaker and weaker. His condition was getting worse due to the weakness. I requested Bibi Ji to come to the hospital with me to give him blessings for life and good health. At that time, he was forty two years old and there were four sisters and two brothers in our family. I was the eldest child in the family. She got ready and came with me to the hospital. She gave him parshad of sugar candies, which he ate right away. She did some simran and said, "He will be out of the hospital and will come home soon." After three days he was released from the hospital. I somehow managed to get him to Bibi's house the next day. She was sitting in meditation for hours. After the meditation, she asked her sister in law to pluck one papaya (a fruit) from the tree from her backyard. Bibi had planted this tree by herself sometime ago. So when she got the yellow papaya Bibi Ji gave it to my dad. She asked him to eat it there. My dad ate the whole papaya. She blessed him and said, "Hazur has given you new life. One day you will play with your grand children."

After two hours my father and I returned back home. Like before, the next morning I went to see Bibi Ji. When I entered her house, she laughed and said, "Look Raj, at night the storm came and uprooted the papaya tree. All the raw papayas were on the ground because your dad got the gift of a long life. The tree from which he ate the papaya has given its own life to your dad. Now you take all these raw papayas for him and cook one everyday to make a vegetable dish. Day by day with the grace of Hazur he will gain more energy and better health." That was the miracle she performed for my dad. Since then, he did not fall sick like that. He died at the age of eighty two and played with his grandchildren. In the same month my Satguru, Sant Kirpal Singh Ji came to Amritsar for a satsang. When he came to know about my dad's recovery, he came to our house to see my dad. My dad told him about Bibi's miracle. At that time, I remember my Satguru Ji told my father that he was blessed with forty years to live, which was correct.

Master Kirpal also used to visit the mental hospital in Punjab, India. One of his initiates, Dr. Leela was the senior doctor of the hospital. She was a very close neighbor of Bibi's house and had high spiritual interests. She used to come to Bibi and used to listen to her satsang and the stories of Hazur. She loved Bibi very much and had a great respect for her. Everyone considered Bibi as the symbol of love. Dr. Leela used to attend Satguru Kirpal Singh Ji's satsang regularly whenever he visited Amritsar. His ashram was next to Bibi's house and right next to Bibi's house was Dr. Lela's residence. She took initiation from Satguru Kirpal Singh Ji and made a lot of progress in her spirituality, being his initiate. She could go to higher regions and used to sit in meditation for a long time. She used to wear a wooden pearled garland around her neck and a wooden bracelet. She always wore dresses that were very simple. Being a student of psychology, I used to go to her house to have tuition classes. She taught me child psychology, normal psychology and abnormal psychology. Sometimes, in order to give practical examples, she used to take me to the hospital where she gave me lessons on the abnormal patients. In brief, due to my spiritual mother Bibi Lajo I was blessed to keep the company of such great personalities of the Punjab.

One day Dr. Leela requested that my Satguru Ji visit the hospital. She told him that there were some mentally ill patients who were very educated. Some of them had been doctors, teachers, professors, businessmen, officers and even ministers. She wanted Satguru to do the satsang for them and give blessings to them. My Satguru Ji agreed to go and decided to visit. One evening when the satsang was done, Satguru Ji was ready to go to the mental hospital. I was standing by his car thinking I will follow him by hiring the auto rickshaw (a three wheeler.) My friend Hem was also standing by me. When my Din Dyal Satguru looked at us he said, "Oh, you are standing there. I was looking for you. Hurry up! Sit in the car." I with joy jumped into the car and so did my friend. Bibi was also there with us in the car. Satguru's driver Mohan started the car and reached the hospital in twenty minutes. When we got out, all the patients were sitting with their fingers on their lips. Some of them were standing at some distance but they also had their fingers on their lips as well. This was an indication that they were not allowed to make noise. Sant Kirpal Singh Ji Maharaj went toward the stage and sat on his chair. The stage was decorated with flowers. Then two patients came with a garland of roses in their hands and tried to put it around the Satguru's neck but Satguru Ji gave a beautiful smile to them and put the same garland around their neck. They were very happy. He then gave a satsang on the topic of the mind and yoga. In his satsang, he called all the patients good souls of yoga. After the satsang, he gave parshad to everyone. It was really a very good scene and no one moved in the satsang. There was silence except the Satguru's voice in the satsang. Some of the patients were singers and musicians, so after the satsang they sang the holy songs of Mira Bai, while the others played the harmonium and the drum. At 9:00 p.m. we came back from the hospital.

In the next month when Satguru Ji came back to Amritsar, Dr. Leela told him that some of the patients were recovering fast. Maharaj Ji said it would take six months for all of them to recover. Their souls are fresh. They did not know about the world much. They are there due to karmas and those who were in the satsang would get well soon. After six months, Dr. Leela came back to Maharaj Ji and informed him that 70 percent of the patients were sent back to their homes and 30 percent were given jobs in the hospital. Such was the greatness of Bibi Lajo, who gave her love to every one through the source of the great Satguru Sant Kirpal Singh Ji Maharaj. I still have details of the satsang which my Satguru gave in the mental hospital. When Maharaj Ji was doing satsang many doctors, officers and the clerks were listening to satsang for the first time and many of them took initiation from Maharaj Ji later on.

MEETING WITH DARSHAN SINGH MAHARAJ JI

Maharaj Darshan Singh Ji had a great love and respect for Bibi Ji. Bibi also loved Maharaj Ji very much. She knew his spirituality since Hazur's time. He was the perfect lover of Hazur as well. When he became Master, I used to travel with her to Kirpal Ashram in New Delhi. When Satguru Darshan Singh Ji Maharaj did satsang for the first time, he met Bibi Ji and gave her full respect. Being a symbol of love, he lovingly folded his hands and thanked Bibi Ji for coming.

In those days the construction of the Ashram was not completely done. So, we stayed in a room at the Ashram for two days. Satguru came to see her and sat for half an hour with Bibi. When he was talking to her I was enjoying his darshan. I was remembering the days when Satguru Kirpal used to sit by her like this and talk in the same way. Sometimes Darshan Singh Ji Maharaj appeared in the form of Satguru Kirpal Singh and I even told Bibi at the same time that Satguru Kirpal Singh Ji is sitting and talking with you. Then Satguru Darshan Singh Ji would show up in his own form and would say to Bibi, "She (me the author) is remembering the Satguru Kirpal." I told him, "No! Satguru Ji is within you." Then he patted me on my back and pressed his soft hand three times on my head and gave the box of sweets as a parshad. This was all due to the great Bibi Lajo. Otherwise I could have never had access to God like that. The days and nights and every moment of my life is spent in her sweet memory. Even today she is supporting me inside and that is why I am around her loving ones.

After his first satsang we came back to the Kirpal Ashram to celebrate Darshan Singh Ji Maharaj's birthday. Both Bibi and I came via train that reached New Delhi at 2:00 p.m. Within an hour, by 3:00 p.m. we reached the ashram. It was very hot and Bibi was very tired and hot. So, I made her sit under the tree by the main gate. I went to ask some sewadars for Maharaj Ji so that I could inform him that Bibi had come with me. Since Bibi was very tired and needed a room to stay and take rest, I was looking for Maharaj Ji. At that time he was busy in the meditation hall which was under construction. I told the sewadar standing at the gate that Bibi Lajo and I had come from Amritsar and Bibi was sitting under the tree and that she was very tired and needed a room in which to rest. I requested him to tell this to Maharaj Ji. He said that he can only tell this when Maharaj Ji comes out of the meditation hall. The rooms were scarce and hard to easily obtain without the permission of Maharaj Ji. But for Bibi Ji he would give a special room and that was why I was forcing the sewadar to go into the meditation hall and give a slip of paper to the Master on which I had mentioned Bibi's predicament. He agreed and put my slip of paper in his pocket. He told me that he would give it to Maharaj Ji in the hall. So, I waited for about five minutes under the hot sun sweating a lot. When he came back he told me that he had given the slip of paper to Maharaj Ji and that he would come to us as soon as he is finished. Since Bibi was waiting under the hot sun and was very tired it was difficult for me to wait for Maharaj Ji. I wanted the Satguru at that time. Inside me was the burning feeling to have his darshan. So, I waited for the best opportunity to talk with Satguru Ji and took advantage of having Bibi with me. Being bold, I forcibly opened the door and asked the sewadar to let me go to the Satguru by myself. During our earlier days, my Satguru Sant Kirpal Singh Ji Maharaj would come out when he would see me. Bibi had already taught me to go to Satguru like this and we had never waited for that long before. As I was struggling with the sewadar at the door, I saw my Satguru Ji coming towards me. He gave a very beautiful smile and asked, "Where is Bibi?" But I asked him, "First let me know, did you receive my slip?" I told him that I doubted in the sewadar who was telling me a lie that he gave my slip to you. My Satguru Ji then told me that he did not receive any message. He said, "If I had received it before then why would I have waited this long?" Then in my ever bold eyes, I looked at the sewadar and said to Maharaj Ji, "You should fire him from this sewa and replace him with me instead." Maharaj Ji Din Dyal, the kind Satguru held my hand and asked me to take him to Bibi Ji, who was watching the whole show from a distance while sitting under a tree. She was laughing at how this stupid lady was able to get to Maharaj Ji and was bringing him to her. When Master himself is pulling your string in his hand he makes all of us play. According to his direction we can do everything. So, Satguru Ji was pulling my string and I was like a puppet. He was making me play with the sewadar. But later when Satguru Ji arranged everything for us I went back to the sewadar brother to apologize for my foolishness. He lovingly said that it was a loving fight between brother and sister. I can even tell the name of my most devoted brother, his name is Mr. Chopra, who loved his sister very much and I can never forget him.

The next day was the celebration of Maharaj Ji's birthday and he did the satsang. Bibi Lajo and I were sitting behind Maharaj Ji. Mata Ji was also there and was wearing a pink dress. She was looking very beautiful. Maharaj Ji stood up and waived his hand to the sangat and gave them his blessing. It was very hot. There were thousands of people who visited for the celebration. There was no place to stand but still the sangat was enjoying his darshan. His face was very bright. It was as bright as the Sun that was shining in the sky at that time. On such a hot day, the sangat even forgot the heat of the Sun when they had the darshan of their Master Darshan Singh Ji.

In the evening, Bibi sent me to Maharaj Ji to convey her message to him that we were leaving for Amritsar the next morning. When I went upstairs, Satguru Ji was sitting in his chair by the porch. In Punjabi you can say *veranda*. He saw me and asked me to sit by him. I sat and gave him the message. Then Mata Ji came with a tray of tea cups for the people who were already sitting with Din Dyal Ji. My Satguru gave me the cup of tea first and gave *burfi* (Indian sweets.) I was very happy to receive the parshad and the beautiful darshan. Then I touched his lotus feet and Satguru Ji placed his hand on my head giving his blessings. When I came in the room and told everything to Bibi, she was very happy to hear this. After one hour, Maharaj Ji and the venerable Mata Ji came in the room to see Bibi.

Maharaj Ji and Mata Ji sat for half an hour. They gave some sewa to Bibi with some boxes of sweets and left the room giving their blessings once again. He gave me a big bag full of sugar candies and cardamoms. Once again, I touched his lotus feet. Mata Ji also gave me her love. It was like a paradise in the room with Bibi, Mata Ji and Satguru Ji all together. All of them were looking like Heavenly grace to me.

HER VISIT TO MASTANA JI ASHRAM (15 MILES AWAY FROM HAZUR'S PLACE)

Bibi Lajo knew everyone who was very dear to Hazur. So, she liked be around them in order to keep the sweet memories of her beloved Master fresh. She welcomed everyone at her house and visited those who loved her very much in the presence of Hazur. They also loved Bibi and were always interested to be in Bibi's company.

In 1982 I visited United States. After four months I came back to India and went to see her. There were some people sitting by her and requesting her to go with them to the Baluchistani Ashram of Mastana Ji located in Sirsa, Hisar. I didn't know these people. I had read about Mastana Ji but I didn't know that there was an ashram. I always kept myself busy in meeting Satguru Kirpal Singh Ji and Darshan Ji or going to Beas. Since my parents and my grandparents were initiated by Hazur; I was brought up in that environment of going to the Beas Dera. Since my childhood I had been going there and I stayed there during my school vacations. I used to do sewa by picking up the baskets full of soil and carrying them on my head, walking two to three miles, throwing down the soil and then I would come back to pick up another one. So like this, I along with my friends and other satsangies used to make several trips doing soil sewa for seven to eight hours every day. I went to Beas whenever I got a chance. I have been going there since 1957 until now.

Now coming back to our story, Bibi agreed to go to the Baluchistani Ashram of Mastana Ji when she saw me. Since I was back from my trip, she looked at me and asked me to get ready. She told me that I'll see another kind of new ashram that will surprise me and I'll never forget this through my life. In fact this statement of hers is still true. The love I've received from the sangat and the Guru, who was also called Manager Sahib by the sangat, is inexpressible. Later, I started calling him Baba Ji and the sangat started calling him Baba Ji too. He was also initiated by Hazur in Beas. Mastana Ji was given the region of Sirsa in the state of Haryana as a responsibility to do the satsang and give initiation in that area. He built the Ashram Sacha Sauda in India and started doing satsang and gave initiation when Hazur was in his physical form. He built a cave by himself for meditation and Hazur came to see the cave. He asked Mastana Ji, "Why have you grown this beard?" as he used to be clean shaven before he left Beas Dera. Mastana Ji answered lovingly that he had grown his beard to use it as a shoe brush for cleaning Hazur's shoes and this made Hazur laugh.

The next day one of my friends and Mastana Ji's initiates, a lady named Pushapa came in the car to take us to the ashram, which was 400 miles away from Amritsar. We reached there at midnight. It took ten hours to drive there. When we reached there all the sangat was waiting for Bibi and gave her a warm reception. She also was there for the first time. They served us with good food and gave us a beautiful room with beautiful beds. In the morning we were called to see Baba Ji. He was surrounded by the sangat and his saint son Maharaj Raghubir Singh Ji, who was initiated by Mastana Ji when he was a little kid. He played in the lap of Mastana Ji. He is bhramchari (unmarried) and devotes his time in meditation and simran all the time. He is also a charming spiritual saint. The devotee Gurdas and Waqil Sahib (who is the successor of Baba Ji) was also there. Baba Ji was the successor of Mastana Ji. He was a complete saint. He welcomed Bibi by putting a garland around her neck and touched her feet even in spite of her stooping to touch his feet, he did it all the same.

Over there the satsang was done at night under the roof of stars and was continued up to late at night. The best singer sang the Kawalian, the classical and typical songs (Bhajan) in praise of Hazur giving reference of Mastana Ji with Hazur's grace to them. At night they were celebrating the birthday of Hazur and they sang all the holy Kawalian songs, playing the harmonium (a musical instrument) and drums in a very rhythmic fashion. Some of the kids even started dancing on the stage along with some men that were intoxicated with the love and grace of the Master. It went on until 2:00 a.m. We stayed for one week and every night we enjoyed the satsang and the songs and Kawalian (these are the typical holy songs sung in Baluchistan with musical instruments.) Everyday Baba Ji used to come in the room to see Bibi Lajo and listen to Hazur's stories from Bibi. Since then, whenever there was a celebration of Hazur's birthday we used to go there along with Bibi. There used to be a numberless sangat when Manager Sahib was doing satsang. **Bibi, the Manager Sahib, Mastana ji and Hazur were living all together.** It was a wonderful connection that teaches us how much love was blessed to them when Hazur was present in his physical form. What an environment and atmosphere would it be in Beas Dera in the days when everyone was living there in the company of Hazur. Later, I continued to go there for many years. Even now, whenever I visit India; I never miss having a visit to the ashram. I have the same love from my satsangi brothers and sisters.

39

MEETING WITH MAHARAJ CHARAN SINGH JI

Bibi eventually started going back to her real home as she knew that she had to go back to her Lord. When Charan Singh Maharaj Ji (new Master in Beas) came to know about her visit in Beas, he arranged a very good room in the guest house which was closer to his residence. She stayed for ten to fifteen days.

I used to complain to her that she was always helping the sangat to have the good darshan of Hazur at her time but why was she not doing this for me. I was very interested to have Charan Singh Maharaj Ji's darshan closely. Once, she went to see Maharaj Ji in his residence. I was with her. We sat in the porch as the sewadar directed us that Maharaj Ji was coming. He came and sat on his chair in front of Bibi. He greeted her saying, "Buaji, I am very happy to see you here. Now you stay here in Beas. I will take care of you." She said, "I can have the darshan of Hazur in you and he told me to come and see you." Both were laughing and talking. I was enjoying good darshan of Maharaj Ji. Then she introduced me to Maharaj Ji. We stayed for fifteen minutes with him. He held Bibi's hand and made her sit in the car. Maharaj Ji asked me to hold her from the other side. So, I was holding her on her left side and Maharaj Ji was holding her from her right side and we were walking slowly and slowly taking her to the car. Then he made her sit in the car and gave a sweet smile to her and looked at me and said to me, "Take care of her and stay here as long as she wants; after all this is her real house." After Maharaj Dyal said these golden words he then told the driver to drive to the guest house. We stayed for fifteen days and Maharaj Ji used to see her everyday. He used to advise her not to go back to Amritsar and said that this was the time for her to stay in her own house. Unfortunately, she came back and her health started going downhill. She told me to go to Beas and tell Maharaj Ji, "Send a car for me and I want to go to Beas because my final time of life has come." I quickly caught the bus for Dera Beas and went to Maharaj Ji's residence. I told the sewadar that Bibi had sent me to convey her message to Maharaj Ji. He was so nice to me that he said, "Just stay here, Maharaj Ji is coming soon." As we were talking, Maharaj Ji Din Dyal Satguru came in a car and stopped the car close to me. He opened the window and asked me if *Buaji* was keeping good health. I replied with tears in my eyes that she had requested him to send a car as she wanted to come to the Dera. Maharaj Ji called the *sewadar* and ordered him to send two sewadars and a car to bring Buaji here. I came back in the same car.

When I reached Amritsar, she was admitted to the hospital. The next morning she was leaving all of us. Maharaj Ji called Dr. Bawa and told him that, "*Buaji* had already gone. I am sending an ambulance which will come at 11:00 a.m. Bring her even if she has oxygen in her. She should be brought directly to the Dera, but not to her own residence in Amritsar. I have arranged everything for her here." The ambulance came at 11:00 a.m. and we sat in the ambulance with Bibi. When we reached the Dera a large part of the sangat was standing in big and long lines. They were all waiting for her last visit in her home. Everybody was saying, "Now, she is back to her final home of her father." The sewadars were arranged everywhere for her last ceremony by her dear Hazur in the form of Maharaj Charan Singh Ji.

When she was given a bath she was dressed with Hazur's white coat over her body and was taken to the grave which was already made by the sewadars on the order of Din Dyal Maharaj Charan Singh Ji. He himself did the ceremony and the pathy (the reciter of the poem) recited a shabad written by Soami Ji. He sang the *shabad.* The words of the *shabad* were: *"Dham apney chalo Bhai."* After he was done Maharaj Ji told her nephew to put fire on the pyre and he did so.

At that time, Bibi's face was red and she was looking alive. I was sitting close to the lotus feet of Din Dyal Satguru Ji. He was not wearing his shoes. He was wearing a white *kurta* and white pajamas and an off white turban. He was looking so beautiful that I have no words to write for him. My younger sister was also sitting with me and all the members of Bibi's family and her dear sangat from Amritsar were also around. There was a numberless sangat watching the whole scene from a distance. Later Maharaj Ji folded his hands and bowed his head to Bibi and left.

So it was a wonderful end to her life and she was sent to Sachkhand by the Great Maharaj Ji Charan Singh. In this way the holy soul of the perfect disciple of Hazur left us, leaving her good and sweet memories and leaving behind a wonderful example.

HER CONNECTION WITH THE GREAT PURI FAMILY

Bibi spoke of the Puri family which was very dear to Hazur. She always told me that the families who were living in the company of Hazur were the great ones who were called Puri by their last name. They settled in Beas Dera first of all. Even the construction of Sachkhand was not started. When Hazur planned the whole design of the building this was the family who took part in sewa for the building. They were the perfect disciples of Hazur. They were doing every kind of sewa. They were managing everything in the Dera. They believed in high thinking of the spiritual path and simple living in the company of their Master. So many retired officers belonging to this family settled in Beas Dera. They had the full devotion and true love for Hazur. They liked to attend the satsang and to have the darshan of their Guru everyday. That was the golden period of their life to be with their loving Guru all the time. When Hazur left his physical form in 1948 there were numberless families who were living in Beas Dera. Their children and the grandchildren studied in the cities and became the top officers by the grace of their Guru. They were coming regularly to attend the satsang of Hazur. They were spending their vacations in the company of their Satguru. Most of them were initiated by Hazur. Most of them got married in the presence of Hazur in Dera Beas. Many were government employees, businessmen, political leaders and ministers. Even the prominent saints of different creeds were coming to attend the satsang of the Great Master. The rich and the poor, the high caste and the low caste people were coming and staying there to do sewa. I am writing because Bibi told me all about her time spent among these people and doing sewa for them. She was helping the people to get initiation from Hazur and whenever they were refused by Hazur she would make the request to Hazur and Hazur would never refuse her. This is a fact because most of the satsangies who were visiting her in my presence would tell how they were helped by Bibi. Most of the Puri family was doing sewa by writing books with Radha Soami stories in connection with Soami Ji Maharaj Ji and Baba Jaimal Singh Ji. They were the first to write such books.

So, Ishwar Puri is specially blessed by his ancestors and the Great Master Hazur Baba Sawan Singh Maharaj Ji who is called "Sachey Patshah" which means the spiritual king of the truth. His grandfather, his father and his paternal uncle Janak Puri all of whom I myself personally knew, all visited my house in Amritsar. They were the main writers of the holy books in connection with Masters in their time and before. They did sewa in the publication of the books. There is a lot to write about them but I am just giving the introduction only. The other families were the Mehata family who were devotees of Hazur. They also had the true love for their Guru. The Sandhu family whom I know myself and spent my time with their relatives later and were the perfect sewadars in handling the administration of the Dera.

The Beas Dera became the center of a spiritual town. All the disciples came from far and wide and liked to stay in the Dera. Some were interested in doing sewa there and wanted to stay there permanently. Slowly these families, with the help of Hazur built rooms and small houses. The satsangies would come to the satsang and spent some days and did a lot of sewa for the construction of the satsangghar. They were staying in the rooms and then went back to their towns. Such was the routine during Hazur's time. Later there were thousands and thousands of sangat and many houses and guest houses were constructed. Today the same Dehra is a big walled city with every type of security there. Numberless guest houses were built by the grace of Hazur.

Ishwar Puri was doing the sewa of picking the souls and taking them to the Dera to show them the spiritual world of his Guru who blessed him at every step of his life in spite of meeting difficulties himself. But the grace of Hazur is always there for him. Now in the Dera, twenty four hours a day the food is free as langar, which was started during Hazur's time. Free hospitals and free dispensaries are there also and people do sewa with love and devotion. Bus stands, taxi stands, and parking are well managed by the managing committee in the Dera. The buildings are built in a modern style. Every modern facility is there.

So, one of the great personalities whom Bibi loved the most was her son Ishwar Puri who was brought up in the lap of Hazur during her time with Hazur. She was respected and loved by his family during Hazur's time. Even later when I was traveling with her we visited some of the families. She told me that the name "Ishwar" was given by Hazur and it means God. He was awakened by Hazur at a young age. He had a firm faith in his Guru and did not miss his satsang even though he was busy in his studies or work. He got the spiritual reflection and the spiritual thoughts as a gift from his loving Guru. The arrows of love pierced his mind so deeply that today he is forced to do his sewa by guiding the good souls on the path of his loving Guru who is always working behind him.

When he was in high posts such as Magistrate, Commissioner of Police, Commissioner of the State and the Chief Secretary of the big state of Punjab, he never forgot to help the needy ones and always was ready to do his Guru's sewa by helping the people working under him. Bibi herself was the witness of his great deeds. He used to visit her under his tight security force of Punjab police. My dad was a police inspector working under him. He knew him very well. Wherever he went, Masters grace was with him. Bibi and he would sit in Hazur's room and would talk about Hazur for a long time. The mother and son were sitting together while a lot of satsangies were staying outside waiting for him so that they could tell him their problems through the intercession of Bibi.

I used to visit his mom and loving sisters sometimes in Beas and in Delhi with Bibi. Sometimes Bibi would send me with some gifts to give to his mom. She was a spiritual lady. She could tell the things which were to come. I can tell my own experience. Once she was not feeling well and Bibi sent me to Delhi from Amritsar five hundred miles away. She gave some sweets as a parshad (blessed food) for her. When I reached there it was about 3 p.m. I had not rung the bell yet. I was standing in the intense heat in the month of July. His mom was lying in her room and called her daughter and told her to run to the door because Raj from Amritsar was standing at the door in the sunshine. She had brought parshad from Bibi. When I saw his sister coming to the door I was surprised. I laughed and asked how she came to know that somebody was at the door when I had not rung the bell yet. She was so happy to see me and opened the door and told me that mom already had sent me to open the door for you. She already knew that you were standing at the door and had parshad for her from Bibi. She took me in her room where her mom was lying on her bed. Looking at me with her shining eyes she took my hand in her soft hand and blessed me. I sat on her bed and she asked me for the parshad sent by Bibi. She said that Hazur had told her about my visit.

I also was blessed by her to do some sewa for her when she was staying in Beas. She was a very loving soul and was blessed by Hazur. I cannot forget her love given to me for some months. When the day came for Bibi's physical departure his sister told me that he called Master Charan Singh Ji and said that Bibi was already with Hazur and that she should be brought to Beas where Maharaj Ji had already made arrangements for her in the Beas Dera. He was calling from the U.S. at 5:00 a.m. Indian time. So it is hard to understand the perfect disciples of the Perfect Master. They do not make the pomp and show of their doings or their hidden love for their Master and neither must they show their spirituality. They can be judged only by their deeds and sewa doing their best for the Master. They like to keep the memories of their Master fresh with them by preaching their teachings and doing well for others. They do sewa with love and devotion and like to teach the same way to others. If someone does not like them then that is their karmas. But the true disciples follow the path of their Master and like to show others.

The holy saint Guru Nanak says, "I would sacrifice myself for the person who recites the name of the Guru by himself and makes others to recite." So we all should follow the saying of Guru Nanak Dev Ji. When the true devotee surrenders himself to his loving Master he has no fear and no worry of Kal (the negative power) because he has the true faith in Him and whatever he does he does with His inner permission. It is written in the holy books that without His order no leaf can move. Whatever one has to do it is written in his destiny before. One who is destined to do His work has to do it and He, the Master himself gets the work done by his loving disciples.

NOTE FOR THE
DEAR READERS

There might be mistakes in grammar but I tried to make it very simple not caring for good vocabulary. I only wanted to tell the satsangie brothers and sisters how Bibi Lajo was dear to Hazur and how she won the heart of her Guru and this task is very difficult for us to surrender ourselves completely in the service of the Master and also to show how to lead the life on the path of the Master. She sacrificed her worldly life for the sake of her Perfect Master and became a perfect disciple of her beloved Master. Not only I, but you can ask anybody who is an old initiate of any Master during her time and they will tell you more than I did. I only lived with her for thirty years. I wrote very briefly about her but she had numberless qualities and skills to make her Master happy and satisfied and she was gifted with more and more virtues which we can never even dream of them to obtain.

Once again I apologize for the mistakes in the book and please try to understand the personality of the holy lady Bibi Laj Wanti, her original name, as she was called Lajo and Kako by her Master Hazur Sawan Singh Maharaj Ji (Kako means "my dear child.")

But the sangat started calling her Bibi Lajo which means "the respected sister Lajo." "Bibi" is a word which shows respect to an elderly woman in the house and the family. She had the only family which was the dear sangat of Hazur. Then the sangat from everywhere she did not even try to know which Master they belonged to and she was only giving her love to them.

Written by the slave of the readers of the dear sangat
R.K. Rajput